CRAIG EVERETT

The Emmaus Road Trip

A Spiritual Journey of discovery and Renewal on Two Wheels

You will seek me and find me when you
seek me with all your heart.

Jeremiah 29:13

Contents

Chapter 1   1
Introduction   1
Chapter 2   6
A Great Redemption Story   6
Chapter 3   10
Just Crazy Enough to Do What God Tells Us to Do   10
Chapter 4   14
Simple Joys   14
Chapter 5   18
This Is My Church   18
Chapter 6   21
Foolish, Weak, Lowly and Despised   21
Chapter 7   25
Feed My Sheep   25
Chapter 8   30
Heaven's Way Biker Church   30
Chapter 9   39
A Tale of Two Churches   39
Chapter 10   49
Lost and Found   49
Chapter 11   55
Mission Waco – Mission World   55
Chapter 12   60
A Slice of Heaven   60

Chapter 13   65
    Truth or Consequences   65
Chapter 14   71
    Lessons Learned   71
Chapter 15   77
    The Biggest Lesson   77
Epilogue   81
Notes   85
About the Author   86

Chapter 1

Introduction

A few years ago, I found myself at a significant crossroad in my life. I was in crisis and struggling to know what to do and which way to turn. I was a husband to Janet and father of six wonderful children, of whom I couldn't have been more proud. By vocation, I was a minister, called by God to proclaim the message of the gospel and help people find new life in God, through Christ, and now my life was falling apart. For the previous 29 years I had been a pastor, church planter and compassionate ministry director, serving homeless men in recovery from alcohol and substance abuse and addiction. Janet and I had even opened our home as licensed therapeutic foster parents, on the surface things still looked pretty good but somewhere a crack or two (or several) were developing and widening in the foundation and suddenly, mine was the life that was falling apart.

As the opening to the 70's television show, The Odd Couple put it: "On November 13th, Felix Unger was asked to remove himself from his place of residence – that request came from his wife." Aside from the date, I received a similar request, though instead of moving in with a childhood friend, I moved back to my childhood home. My father had died a few years prior to this event so mom was alone and happy for the company, though devastated in her own way by the circumstances.

With all the upheaval in my personal life, my work life suffered and the ministry I had been leading for the past eleven years was now struggling financially. As I worked to develop the budget for the coming fiscal year, I just couldn't make the numbers work. No matter how hard I tried to trim and scrimp, I couldn't get the expenses to line up with the projected income. I knew I needed to either dramatically cut expenses or find a new source of income and since the lead time on new funding sources can take several months to develop, I was left with no good alternatives. As I examined the budget, I came to realize that my salary as the Executive Director was the largest single line item in the expense column, so, believing the continuation of the ministry was more important than who the Director was, I decided to fire myself. I informed the Chairman of the Board of my decision (the entire board was already aware of my personal crisis and had been kept apprised of the financial situation) and we worked together to make my exit as smooth as possible.

I took a job in sales, as that had been my career prior to ministry and started to try to rebuild my life and repair my marriage. Unfortunately, the hits just kept coming. While I was away at a two-week training for the new job, my mother who had been suffering with some significant hip and back pain, was diagnosed with bone cancer, and given very little hope for cure or remission. For the next six months, I watched as the woman who had given me life, slowly and painfully lost hers.

As awful as the situation was, there was a strange blessing to it. My only sibling, my sister, lived just a short distance away and had recently retired. Between the two of us, we were able to provide twenty-four-hour care for mom and while we had visiting nurses from a local hospice agency, there wasn't a single minute in the last three months of her life that either my sister or I weren't there with our mother. Had the other crises not been happening in my life would I have had the blessing of caring for my mother the way I was able to do? Doubtful. Though I don't buy into the adage that everything happens for a reason, I do believe the Bible when it says: "And we know that in all things God works for the good of those who love him, who have been called according to his purpose."

A couple of months after mom's passing, however, I found myself feeling very discontent, realizing that Janet and I weren't making any progress in healing our marriage and that things seemed to be getting worse. I went to visit my old friend Steve one evening and as we sat in his living room sharing a bottle of scotch (full disclosure – while I'm not at all a big drinker, I am most definitely not a scotch drinker, but desperate times and all...) out of the blue I declared, "Stephen, I need a new quest." For the next hour or so we tossed about various ideas, most of which were utterly ridiculous, but that's what brainstorming often is right? One thing I made clear as we talked is that while part of me just wanted to run away from all my problems, I really wanted to run toward something; I didn't want to escape my suffering, I wanted it to have a purpose. Eventually I said, "You know, I've been in pastoral ministry for nearly thirty years now, and while I have seen many lives touched and improved, I have seen very few instances of people radically transformed. I've been thinking about doing something crazy like hopping on my motorcycle and hitting the road in search for God in America today and blogging about what I find." Stephen bolted upright in his chair, snapped his fingers, pointed at me, and said, "That's it." I said, "What do you mean, 'that's it', you don't even believe? Why would you say I should go in search of God in America and write about it?" "Because I, unbeliever that I am, would be interested in reading about what you find." For the next hour or two we brainstormed this one idea, and the seed and excitement began to grow.

A day or two later I was at the racetrack with another old friend who races go-karts. Jim and I have known each other since we were five years old and oddly our earliest connection was centered around racing. My father worked for the company Jim's father owned, and our dads' raced sports cars in the Sports Car Club of America (SCCA). Jim had invited another high school chum, Keith, whom I hadn't seen in many years and as we sat catching up, while Jim was taking practice laps around the track, I shared my rough plan with him. Similarly, he indicated that though he wasn't very religious, considering himself more of an agnostic, he too would be interested in following along with what I discovered in my journey. Having been affirmed by two different secular sources, I decided to share my idea with some of my Christian colleagues and solicit their prayers. Receiving further affirmation and the promise of their prayers from several clergy and laymen, the real planning began in the summer of 2014.

What follows in this book is more than just a travelogue. While much of what you will read is a compilation of some of the blog posts I wrote while traveling, each is intended to record a little bit about how I saw a reflection of Christ in the people I met on my journey. I hope you will find these encounters uplifting and that you will stay with me to the end of the book as I seek to apply the lessons I learned along the way.

A Note on the title of this book, the blog, and the journey:

I have long been enamored with the story of Cleopas and his un-named companion as they walked from Jerusalem to the little town of

Emmaus on that first Easter Sunday. Even as I write this, a painting of this scene, painted for me by my mother, hangs above my desk. The record of this event is found in the 24th chapter of the gospel of Luke and we are told that "They were talking with each other about everything that had happened. As they talked and discussed these things with each other, Jesus himself came up and walked along with them; but they were kept from recognizing him." (Luke 24:14-16) What strikes me so about this story is how these spiritually hungry, yet broken, people encountered Christ in a most unusual and totally unexpected way. Since I love the story of the Emmaus Road and was about to embark on an extended road trip in search of Christ, with the expectation of finding Him in unexpected places (if that even makes sense) I decided to call my journey The Emmaus Road Trip: A Search for the Reflection Christ in Postmodern North America.

Chapter 2

A Great Redemption Story

The Traversy Family

On my way south I made one of my few planned stops in Thomasville, NC to catch up with the Traversy family. Genevieve Traversy was the very first foster child we welcomed into our home several years ago. In the years that followed we welcomed five more, each memorable in their own way, yet no other has made more out of their lives and difficult beginnings than Genevieve.

When Genevieve came to live with us shortly after her 16th birthday, she arrived with an open, indomitable spirit – and her two-week old son. As I sat in her living room the other night, she told me that ours was at least the twelfth home she had been placed in during her years in the foster care system. [Genevieve and her story have been featured in NH Division of Children Youth and Families conferences; a video produced by DCYF can be seen on YouTube at the following address - https://youtu.be/2KBz9qjHC6s] With a history such as hers, most people would flounder and fall into despair and addiction or worse. But God had his hand on Genevieve and wrought redemption in and through her life. Though she was in many ways a typical rebellious teenager, it was clear that there was something special about Genevieve. Even at an age when most kids were into music and fashion, she was a devoted mother caring for her infant son with a tenderness not often seen. She managed the middle of the night feedings and changings and still kept up with her schoolwork, even though coming to a new home meant registering at yet another new school. When we told her that we attended church every Sunday (I was after all, the pastor of a church plant at the time) she was happy to hear it and gladly attended church with our family, always open to the word of God, which had been established in her heart at an early age. Though she lived with us for only about a year, I am grateful to God that we have stayed in touch and been privileged to witness His hand in her life.

A few years back Genevieve called me to ask if I would perform her marriage to Shawn. I responded as I usually do to such requests, saying that I only do Christian weddings so I would need meet with she and her fiancé at least six times to explain what a Christian marriage is all about. To my surprise she told me that Shawn wanted that, so it was my distinct pleasure and honor to take Genevieve and Shawn through premarital counseling and joining them as husband and wife. During that counseling, I shared the truth of the Gospel with Shawn, and while I believe he accepted the message intellectually, he would admit that he didn't actually cross the line of faith until months later when they got plugged in to a wonderful church. Today, Genevieve and Shawn are parents to four wonderful children and oh what tremendous growth and transformation can be seen in this entire family.

When I showed up at their doorstep, I was welcomed with warm greetings and hugs. Genevieve had been busy most of the day, teaching at a homeschool co-op, and Shawn had been working on their ailing family van, but there was no sense that I was inconveniencing them in any way. They have a home where all are welcome. In fact, hospitality is something they practice regularly and though far from wealthy in a material sense, they are willing and eager to share whatever they have with whoever is in need.

Though Genevieve was a ward of the state from a very early age, she always made great effort to stay in touch with her birth family and cultivated relationships with her mother and brothers. As her foster parents, we understood how important those ties are and had welcomed Genevieve's mom to holiday dinners in our home. Years after Genevieve had left our home and I was working with the homeless in Manchester, NH, developing a new collaborative project with several other agencies, I happened to spot a woman stumbling down the middle of the street early one morning. I was forced to slow down for fear she may lurch in front of my car and as I passed her, I had a flash of recognition, it was Genevieve's mom. My heart sank to see her in such a state and thought then of how much pain Genevieve must feel.

That incident took place a year or two before the call about getting married. When I showed up at Genevieve and Shawn's apartment for our second premarital counseling appointment, Genevieve apologized for the mess saying that her mom had recently moved in with them, had accepted Christ, was sober and ready to go into treatment for the first time. Sure enough, there was the same woman I had seen stumbling down the street, standing before me, still looking a little haggard, but bright eyed and clear headed. I am thrilled to say that while I, as one who dealt with alcoholics and drug addicts daily, was a bit skeptical, Genevieve's mom, did go to treatment, got into a transitional housing program and eventually her own place and maintained sobriety from that day forward. I attribute her success to the fact that she believed the power of God to transform lives because she witnessed that power in the transformed life of her daughter.

Those familial relationships that Genevieve fostered – her older brother Jeff, walked her down the aisle and gave her away at her wedding. Sadly, Jeff died last year and his daughter, Kaitlyn, had a very hard time of it. A few months ago, she asked Genevieve if she could come live with her and her family. After praying together, Genevieve and Shawn agreed to have her come. Kaitlyn has also come into a relationship with God as a result of this loving family's example and is flourishing in her new life.

The baby who I first met at two-weeks of age is now almost 16. He is smart as a whip and taking college courses offering credits toward his high school diploma. He will likely complete his home education and graduate soon. He is extremely tech savvy and is producing music and music videos of amazing quality. His younger siblings are excelling in their own rights (congratulations again to Kahleb, whose football team just completed their second undefeated championship season) and like so many homeschooled siblings I have known, have their squabbles but are clearly devoted to one another. This entire family stands as a wonderful testimony to God's amazing grace and reflect the nature, character of love of Jesus in virtually everything they do.

Thank you Traversy's for offering a place to lay my head for the night and sharing your lives with me.

Just Crazy Enough

Chapter 3

Just Crazy Enough to Do What God Tells Us to Do

Ray and Susan Kelley

After a week of reading, writing, reflecting, and riding around the Daytona Beach area in search of something that really stands out as worth exploring, I was coming up empty.

Since I said I was trusting God to lead in this adventure, I decided there was no sense in feeling frustrated and figured I just needed to roll with it. I decided to look for some live music and just kick back for a Friday evening. Well, God leads in mysterious ways as they say. A Google search for "live music Daytona Beach" returned information about wild looking nightclubs, biker bars, dives, and a coffee shop called Jakob's Well. Hmmm, that looked promising, so I clicked and found myself at the website for Daytona Outreach Center, a ministry that provides rehab and housing for homeless addicts. Digging around, I found an interesting looking program that was no nonsense discipleship. I fired off a quick email to the founders but decided to pop on over to the coffee shop since was less than a mile from where I was staying.

While I was chatting with the man at the counter, Susan walked out of the backroom, overheard me, and said she had just received my email. She then introduced me to Tim, the coffee shop manager and what a story he had to tell. It seems that he was a homeless addict just walking the streets a couple years ago when Susan's husband, Ray, pulled him aside. Ray asked a simple question of Tim. "If I offered you a place to live with no strings attached accept that I would also teach you about Jesus, would you like that?" Tim asked for a few minutes to think about it, went and smoked a cigarette and came back to Ray after about ten minutes and agreed to the simple terms. That was over two years prior, and Tim never touched drugs again. He now follows the same simple discipleship process of watching the crowds at various gatherings, asking the same basic question of guys he feels the Lord leading him to speak with. Some look at him like he's a bit crazy, but others respond much as he did. Over the past several years hundreds of homeless addicts have found hope through this ministry and now both Jakob's Well and The Daytona Outreach Center Thrift Store are managed and operated by men who have been through the discipleship program.

Later that evening I went back for the live music and Tim introduced me to Ray Kelley, the man who started it all. Ray sat and shared his story with me for the next two hours. He had been a successful businessman but hung with a rough biker crowd and got into methamphetamines. After their "chef" got busted, Ray became the new meth chef and set up a mobile lab, a la Breaking Bad. Susan was a good Christian wife who made sure her family got to church every Sunday but in a moment of weakness, she finally gave in to Ray's invitation to try a taste of meth. One try was all it took and for the next five years Ray and Susan lost everything they had. Over one 18-month period Ray told me, they burned through $900,000 and didn't buy a single home or car or motorcycle or any major tangible item. They became two homeless addicts who hated each other. They went their separate ways and continued to self-destruct. Eventually, Ray says, he was homeless, helpless, and hopeless and he cried out to God, not for salvation but to take his life. As Ray put it, God's answer to that prayer was, "No." Instead of dying, Ray began to feel just a little bit of peace. Since God didn't strike him dead Ray asked God to deliver him from his addiction and God did just that. From that day, nearly ten years ago, Ray never touched the drug that had ruined his life. He got in line with God's plan and purpose and eventually he and Susan reunited and began ministering to others together.

One Friday night a few months later Ray had been asked to lead a Bible study at a homeless outreach program in Daytona Beach. Ray says instead of leading a Bible Study, he got to preaching to the small group of seven people and while he was preaching, he sensed the Lord telling him to take them all home with him. He said he tried to ignore the voice and kept on preaching – louder to try to drown out the voice he was hearing. But he couldn't quiet the voice. When he was through preaching, he went to Susan and shared with her the sense he had, hoping that she would tell him it was ridiculous and out of the question. Instead, she smiled and said, "Praise God!" Ray protested and knew it wasn't a good idea, but Susan said if it's really God speaking to you, you can't refuse, even if you think it doesn't make sense.

Ray described these seven characters as, two men who were bi-vocational (pimps and drug dealers) three women who were "self-employed entrepreneurs", a teenage runaway and one just plain home-less addict. Oh yes, Ray and Susan also had a 15-year-old daughter still living with them at the time, so they called to prepare her for what they were bringing home. This family of three was suddenly ten living in a three-bedroom house. That first weekend the runaway and one of the pimps took off together, but the other five stayed and were discipled by Ray and Susan. For the rest of our time together Ray shared story after story of the adventure they have been on and God's provision time-after-time (including a recent $10,000 award from CBS and USA Networks in their "Characters Unite" program.) Over the next several years, God provided more homes for little or no money and has lead Ray and Susan to begin these social enterprise programs to provide jobs and generate income for the ministry. Ray admits that what they do is unconventional and in some people's minds, dangerous, but no one argues with the results. Hundreds of homeless addicts have been rescued, discipled, and trained to reproduce. As Ray declared to me, "We're just crazy enough to do what he tells us to do."

As we ended our conversation Ray said, "if you want to see another cool ministry you won't find publicized anywhere, you should check out the Sunday morning service at Sun Splash Park. Every Sunday at 7:00 am, there's a great service for the homeless and the residents of an assisted living facility that's right across the street." We'll come to that experience in a couple chapters.

Chapter 4

Simple Joys

Jakob's Well

One night I was feeling sorry for myself and perhaps a little depressed. I tend to be a glass half-full kind of guy, so usually I can talk myself out of a bad mood but as I have indicated here before, there were certain circumstances of my life that I simply wished were not. So, it was with a slightly downcast spirit that I walked into Jakob's Well, again that evening to check out the open mic/karaoke night.

I arrived just before the advertised start time of 7:00 pm and what I found when I walked through the door set me back on my heels. To put this delicately, I discovered a short-bus load of well… grown up short-bus riders. Okay, maybe that wasn't very delicate. The fact is I have never been politically correct, and I happen to think that some of the pc terminology can be more offensive or confusing than straight talk, but I guess the current language is either "developmentally delayed" or "developmentally challenged." Perhaps as I have heard it's not "developmentally disabled" but "other abled." Whatever terminology you prefer, feel free to do a pc edit in your own mind – I won't be offended.

Now, the reason I rocked back on my heels and took this in so quickly is that two of the challenged folk were up on-stage singing karaoke with far more enthusiasm than their vocal talents warranted. For a moment I wondered if I had stumbled into one of those American Idol first audition deals. While I fear I may have stood agape for too long, I think in reality I processed the scene far more quickly and my slack jaw face turned to a smile in a mere second or two. I continued to absorb and process the scene as I walked to the counter, ordered a coffee, and made my way to a seat.

As I sipped my coffee, my smile broadened (in the interest of full disclosure, I will admit that I was laughing on the inside, but it was not a derisive laughter at all, taking in the whole scene. Please excuse my feeble attempt at painting this picture with words, but imagine if you can, a rail thin man in his thirties with wispy thinning hair and thick glasses, dressed in tight tan shorts, a red t-shirt and shod in converse sneakers, with his hips canted slightly when still, but moving rapidly to the music belting out Alabama's, "Roll on Eighteen-Wheeler, Roll on!"

As soon as he finished his set, he went to the DJ and ordered up a song for one of his compatriots to sing and it became self-evident that this man was the alpha-male of the room. As further proof of this fact, since the song now being sung was a slow song, I watched as he went to the girl who was clearly "his woman" and led her to the dance floor. As they swayed in rhythm to the music, her head on his chest, I was enthralled. Just when I thought I was witnessing the epitome of simple, joyous love, she leaned back, gazed longingly in his eyes, and he bent to give her the sweetest kiss I think I have ever seen. Nicholas Sparks could not capture with words what I saw with my own eyes.

Well, the night was still young, and I began to ponder what else was in store. I was quite certain I had been told that a regular crowd of un-churched folks came to perform for open mic and as some of them began to shuffle in I kind of wondered how they would respond to the group that was already there. What would this interaction look like? Would there be disgust? Would there be a clear distinction between the "normal" people and the "challenged" folks. Would the room be evenly divided and segregated? Would there be rivalry? How would the staff keep order since it had been pretty much a free for all to this point? Perhaps it was my previous mood that conjured up these negative speculations but any fears of tensions I held were quickly put to rest, for the interaction between the haves and have nots was one of casual comfort and mutual respect.

I watched as a hipster dude with a baldpate, partially hidden beneath a fedora, and neatly trimmed goatee warmly greeted the alpha-male. This was clearly not the first time these two groups had mingled. While the karaoke continued, Mr. hipster dude tuned his guitar, waiting patiently for his mic time. When he was ready and it was his turn to perform, along with his buddy on the snare drum, the entire audience listened with rapt attention.

After he played three or four songs, Tim, the manager, announced that he needed a couple volunteers (he wound up with four or five). He instructed his team of volunteers to choose a song – any song – for Tony (one of the guys in the Daytona Outreach Center program) to sing. This was a little game they call "karaoke roulette" and the idea is to find a song that's hard to sing in an effort to embarrass Tony. Alpha-male huddled his troops to discuss the matter and when they broke, he clapped his hands pointed to Tim and said, "Eighteen-Wheeler," the song he had earlier performed. Tony accepted the challenge, but it was painfully clear he did not know the song as well as the previous performer.

While Tony struggled to sing, the music played, and the hipster dude danced across the floor inviting a blond-haired woman with Down's syndrome to join him. Though she was at first flustered, she stepped out and tried to follow his lead. He gently spun her and swung her around the floor, and she began to relax enjoying the attention and doing her best to mimic his moves. The room was filled with an air of pure delight.

Now, some of you might think that Jesus would never dance and make such a spectacle of himself, but I'm pretty sure I saw the reflection of Christ last night.

Authors note: It is difficult to capture all I witnessed, for there was so much more worthy of cataloguing. Yet, I fear that my descriptions of some of the other characters I saw would come off sounding snarky, like I am poking fun when my desire is just the opposite. I truly was taken by the simple joy exhibited by these folks who face life's challenges with their own special kind of dignity. They helped put my problems in perspective, lifted my mood and caused me to give thanks to God for so many good things in my life. It struck me that evening that so often, what we seek is right before our eyes; we simply fail to perceive it, just like Cleopas and his companion.

Chapter 5

This Is My Church

Jeremy Folmsbee

At Ray Kelley's suggestion, I rose early on Sunday to seek out this beachside homeless church he told me about. Fortunately, I didn't have far to go and didn't have to look too hard. By God's grace, and thanks to the generosity of friends, Jen and Bill, I was staying at their place just off Silver Beach Ave. and Sun Splash Park is about a mile east and then north on Atlantic Ave. The weather was cool and drizzly as it seemed to be on so much of my trip and I was glad for the short ride looking through the rain drops on my visor that wanted to fog no matter how much anti-fog treatment I applied.

As I pulled into the parking lot I spotted a rag-tag group of people gathering loosely around various playground apparatus and figured, this must be the place. It didn't look like any church I had ever been to, there were no pews or chairs, no altar, candles or offering plates, no piano or any other form of a keyboard, though I did spot one young man with a guitar case and I could only guess what might be inside and though I am no musician, I know that it's hard to keep a guitar in tune in the cold and damp. As I approached, I tried to pick out the person who seemed to be in charge, assuming he would be the pastor to this rather motley looking group. I immediately ruled out the man wearing a football helmet as well as the man who reminded me of the Gorton's fisherman and those hunched over walkers with tennis ball slides. Finally, I spotted a man near to my age who was wiping off the slides and swings and benches in the area. I introduced myself and told him that Ray had sent me. He was very gracious and welcoming, and we chatted a bit while he worked. We had been talking for several minutes when I asked a question about how long this church had been meeting like this and he said' "I don't know, you'll have to ask the pastor, he's around here somewhere, I'll be happy to introduce you." Oops, so much for my skills at discernment. I later got to know this man better and learned he was an attorney and that he and his wife were wonderful servants using their gifts and resources where they were most useful.

Shortly, a much younger looking man came along, and I was introduced to Jeremy. As a pastor, I knew better than to keep him for long before the service and hoped to get a little of his time following whatever was about to take place. As I milled about, I spotted some young adults toting a couple large coffee urns and boxes of Krispy Kreme doughnuts, an older gentleman carrying and passing out bags of bananas and yet another with bags of McDonalds' breakfast burritos. This man it turns out was a retired tugboat captain and had worked the northeastern seaboard, from Maine to New York for any years.

As the 7:00 start time rolled around, the group of about thirty people began to coalesce, huddling together to sing a couple songs and listen to an incredibly well-presented message telling this gathering of variously abled people that they are "the light of the world", (see Matthew 5:14). I was so impressed with Jeremy's ability to preach and engage with his congregation of people who might never feel welcome in any traditional church. He knew them all by name and ability and managed to communicate a deep and challenging message with appropriate simplicity.

As we had time to talk after the service, I learned that Jeremy had been a PGA Pro and was an avid surfer. He and his wife were raising their own five children and discipling two of the young people who had carried the coffee urns and lead the singing. Having complimented Jeremy on his message and the work in general, I asked, "Does your church help support this work in the park?" He stepped back a bit, looked me in the eye and declared, "This is my church." He went on to explain that at one time earlier in this work he had been a part of another church and the Sun Splash service had been started as an outreach ministry, but the church tried to control what he did and expected it to be used to draw people to the sponsoring church and when the park people didn't show up in church right away, they felt it was simply a drain on their resources. Then, Jeremy concluded the matter by stating, "The Bible calls us to make disciples, not build churches, and we are making disciples here."

Just as it was with Cleopas when Jesus broke the bread, my eyes were opened, and I recognized the spirit of Christ in this unassuming servant.

Chapter 6

Foolish, Weak, Lowly and Despised

James "Cochise" Powell

My first encounter with Cochise was an interesting happenstance. When I started this trip, I said that I was relying on God to direct my steps and what an adventure it has been. It was a Friday afternoon in Daytona Beach, and I had yet to find much in the way of unique, effective ministries. I had decided to try to enjoy my evening and began a search for some live music. That's when I found Jakob's Well and met Ray and Susan Kelley, whose story I already wrote in chapter 2, "Just Crazy Enough to Do What He Tells Us to Do." Ray told me about Jeremy Folmsbee from the previous chapter, it was at that service that I met Pace Allen, a Christian Attorney, who invited me to a men's prayer breakfast at First Baptist Church. Following the breakfast and a study on God and Country, I found a group of five or six men chatting about spiritual things and decided to pull up a chair. Sitting across the table from me was a man who was clearly looked to as an authority by the others in the circle. He was dressed casually with a black driving cap on backwards atop his longish salt and pepper hair, sporting a neatly trimmed goatee with tattoos up and down both arms. This was my first encounter with Cochise, and I immediately sensed a need to talk further with him about my mission.

I left Daytona later that day headed to Virginia to celebrate Thanksgiving with two of my sons. When I returned a few days later I decided to attend Cochise's service at Set Free Church. Though not specifically a "Biker Church" Set Free is a church that is geared toward reaching those who might not feel comfortable in a more traditional church. I was warmly greeted at the door and walked into a meeting room with about 25-30 people milling about and settling in for the service. For me, the service was oddly nostalgic, taking me back to my own church planting days. I say "oddly nostalgic" because I don't always look back with fondness on those often, difficult days. However, somehow already on this journey, I am seeing the organic nature of that work in a very different light.

For those of you who perhaps haven't been to church in a while, things have changed. As a child in a mainline church, we always had a choir. When I went back to church (an "evangelical" church) in the late 70's I found the same formula with which I grew up, albeit a little more upbeat and less somber. Nowadays, most contemporary churches have a "worship band" instead of a choir and the words of the songs are projected on the wall or a giant screen in lieu of hymnals. In church planting, however, you must be creative and work with what you've got. Set Free Church uses a laptop and projector with recorded music. We sang along to old songs like "Victory in Jesus" "I'll Fly Away" along with other Christian classics. It just felt good to a middle-aged guy with a bass voice who sometimes struggles with the modern stuff that seems written for men with a higher range. if for men at all.

At Set Free Church the people were friendly, casually dressed and appeared well aware of their shortcomings; there was no pretense and no facades. The message was solidly Biblical, and Cochise was very engaging with his congregation. The music was familiar and the fellowship warm and inviting. In my spirit, I sensed the presence of Christ.

When I ran into Cochise a day or two later and told him I was struggling with what to write about him, he was quick to say, "I don't know that you will see the reflection of Christ in me, unless it's in the call to be broken." Well, as a matter of fact, I do see the reflection of Christ in that call, furthermore, I see the reflection Christ in his humility and desire to reach those who might not feel comfortable or even welcome in many churches today.

As further evidence of his desire to reach those who may be disenfranchised from traditional forms of worship, on the fourth Sunday of every month, Set Free Church meets early so they can conduct an additional service at Boot Hill Saloon, a popular biker bar amongst several such bars along Main Street in Daytona. Thanks to the relationships that have been built at Boot Hill, Cochise was invited to conduct a Christmas Eve candlelight service. Though I had already gone south, I decided it was worth a few extra miles to be able to attend that service, so as I headed north in preparation for my westward journey, I cut back across Florida in order to enjoy this unique setting for the celebration of the birth of Christ.

Thanks to this servant of God, I have also had the pleasure of meeting his friend Bobby Wells in Fort Myers, who sent me to see Robert Happoldt, pastor of Heaven's Way Biker Church in Cottondale, Florida, to whom I will introduce you in chapter seven. This network of unconventional, ambassadors for Christ has been a wonderful blessing to me on my journey and opened my eyes further to the truth of 1 Corinthians 1:26-30 which reads: "Brothers and sisters, think of what you were when you were called. Not many of you were wise by human standards; not many were influential; not many were of noble birth. But God chose the foolish things of the world to shame the wise; God chose the weak things of the world to shame the strong. God chose the lowly things of this world and the despised things—and the things that are not—to nullify the things that are, so that no one may boast before him. It is because of him that you are in Christ Jesus, who has become for us wisdom from God—that is, our righteousness, holiness and redemption."

Chapter 7

Feed My Sheep

Keys Vineyard Church

Having spent far longer in the Daytona area than I intended, I was beginning to think this wasn't much of a road trip and there were so many other places I wanted to explore and experience and hopefully see the reflection of Christ. I'd left home more than a month before and couldn't believe all the transformed and transforming lives I had already encountered. In hindsight, I'm certain that if I were to ask a hundred people where they would expect to see authentic Christian ministry taking place, not one of them would direct me to Daytona Beach, Florida. I am further convinced that not one out of thousands would suggest I head to the Florida Keys in my search, nevertheless, that is exactly where the Spirit led me next.

Before leaving New Hampshire, I had a tentative place to stay arranged in Marathon, but as I headed further south and sought to confirm, I learned that my lodgings had fallen through. While I had enjoyed the luxury of Bill and Jen's condo in Daytona, my main plan for overnights had been to camp. I had a great enclosed hammock set-up and all the gear I needed for camping in the saddlebags and strapped to the passenger seat on the bike so all I really required was a couple trees twelve to fifteen feet apart – shouldn't be too hard to find. Well, it's never been a problem in New England, but in the state parks in the Keys, not so. Besides, the camping fees for a most basic sight at Bahia Honda State Park were a minimum of $100.00 per night at the time and I was on a budget. While on the road between Daytona and Miami, I stopped to search for churches in the Keys and fired off an email to a half-dozen of them introducing myself, explaining what I was doing and asking if they might have a place, I could hang my hammock for a few nights. Of those six churches, only one responded to my query. From pastor Steve Lawes at Keys Vineyard Church in Big Pine Key, I receive a very cordial email assuring me they could at minimum find a place where I could hang a hammock and could probably do even better than that for me. He gave me his phone number and told me to call when I hit Big Pine.

I arrived late on a Wednesday afternoon, called as instructed and Steve informed me, they were preparing dinner for the Wednesday night service, gave me directions to the church and told me to come on by anytime. I found a large steel building that looked more like an indoor tennis facility than a church, but the sign assured me I was in the right place. I found someone who directed me to pastor Steve who offered me a warm sincere greeting. He said he had hoped that "Rico" would be around because he had been the chaplain for a local motorcycle club and knew he would be happy to put me up, but since he couldn't find him, I was welcome to stow my gear and sleep in the church's prayer room where there were some comfortable couches. The only thing is he said, when we close up for the night and leave, we'll have to lock you in, but there's a shower upstairs and everything you need. Just make yourself to home and help yourself to some dinner as soon as it's ready. With that he headed off to continue helping to get the dinner ready, I rode my bike around back into a fenced in enclosure, unloaded my bike and brought my sleeping back and necessary items into the prayer room. Once again, I found myself milling around with a group of strangers gathered for fellowship and learning. In the backend of what served as the sanctuary there were a couple dozen round plastic folding tables with chairs set up for the meal and four or five long tables festooned with chafing dishes, large salad bowls and baskets of bread. I took my place in the buffet line when we were all informed that dinner was ready, and the prayer of blessing had been spoken.

With a plate heaping over and a cup of iced tea in hand, I searched the room for an empty seat and a friendly face or two. I spotted a table with three men about my age or a little older and asked if I might join them. They waved me to the only empty chair and welcomed me. Introductions were made all around and I learned that none of those men attended the church, they just showed up every week for the meal and left before the Bible study started.

After dinner Steve found me and introduced me to "Rico", whose given name is John, but since his last name is Petrocelli, he was given the nickname, thanks to the great Rico Petrocelli, shortstop and third baseman for my home team Boston Red Sox and part of the Impossible Dream team of 1967. I was nine years old that year and remember we were allowed to watch the World Series against the St Louis Cardinals in our fourth-grade classroom. Ah, but I digress, this is about the other Rico Petrocelli, who is retired and living in the Keys and is a most gracious host. This Rico greeted me and invited me to stay at his place for as long as I wanted. Since I was all set up in the prayer room, I told him I would stay the night at the church but would be happy to accept his invitation and hospitality starting the next day.

As the saying, attributed to Benjamin Franklin goes, "Guests, like fish, begin to smell after three days." With this in mind I intended to stay no more than three days with Rico, yet he was so gracious, and we had such fun together that I wound up, once again, staying in one place much longer than planned. He lives in a gated mobile home park where all the units are built on stilts as a precaution to the many hurricanes that pass nearby or through the Keys. Some days we rode and toured around together, others he had things to do, and I continued to explore the far reaches of this tropical paradise. Several evenings we sat and talked about spiritual issues and relationships or watched videos about creation and it was one of my most relaxing times in years. I will ever be grateful to this brother in Christ and to the man who introduced us.

During my stay I also had the opportunity to sit and interview Steve about the church and his history with it. Turns out he was one of the eighteen or so founding members of the church that now ran between 800 – 1200 in attendance every week. In an area with a population that fluctuates seasonally between 8,000 and 12,000 residents, that means they are consistently reaching 8 – 10 percent of the local population. If you know anything about church demographics, you will know that if a church can reach 1 percent of its areas population it is doing very well. As we talked a mentioned to Steve the conversation I had with my dining companions a few nights earlier, who came for the food but left before things got spiritual and asked if that was a problem to him or other church leaders. He said it wasn't a problem at all, that the church understands and that they don't do it simply as a hook to get people to come, they do it to serve their community. In fact, they do it, that is serve a meal, at least six times each week; at each of the three Sunday morning services, before the Sunday evening service, before the Wednesday night service, before the other midweek youth service and often for other special events. Food, Steve said represents about

15 – 20 percent of the church's annual budget and they feel it is worth every penny.

When Jesus restored Peter after he had denied even knowing him, three times Jesus asked, "Peter, do you love me?" after his third assertion that yes indeed, Peter loved him, Jesus replied, "Feed my sheep." (see John 21:15-17) We understand that Jesus meant that in a spiritual sense, yet this loving church has taken that command quite literally, feeding their community, filling bellies as well as souls.

Chapter 8

Heaven's Way Biker Church

Robert & Alecia Happholdt

In the original Emmaus Road journey, which is recorded in the Bible in Luke 24, we are told that two disciples were walking along talking about Jesus' arrest, crucifixion the empty tomb and that; "As they discussed these things with each other, Jesus himself, came up walked along with them; but they were kept from recognizing him." (Luke 24:15-16)

Why they failed to recognize him is unknown. Bible scholars and commentators have written a number of possible explanations, but all must admit that the final answer remains elusive. Whether the issue was their vision (or lack thereof) or Jesus possibly altered appearance we do not know. All we know is that "they were kept from recognizing him." It is this very notion, which has been key to my journey. I have been following the leading of the Holy Spirit, praying constantly for "eyes to see" what God is doing in these days and through what people and means.

As earlier chapters have indicated, the people God led me to whom He is using to impact this age in North America, are not people most of us would immediately recognize as reflections of Christ. So it is that we come to another case in point: Robert and Alicia Happoldt and their work at Heaven's Way Biker Church in rural Cottondale, FL.

In 2000, Robert and Alicia were living the hardcore biker's life in southern Alabama, making, doing, and selling drugs. In Alicia's words it was a marriage made in Hell, where abuse and fear were part of her daily life. At that time, Robert was known as "Roger Rabbit" a fast-living man with lots of drugs and a big gun. Occasionally Alicia tried to get away, but Robert always found her and forced her back home. Then one early Wednesday morning in July, the 12th Judicial Circuit Drug and Violent Crimes Task Force came a knocking' with search warrant in hand. It was no gentle knock, really more of a crash, and what the Task Force discovered, resulted in charges of possession and trafficking, earning both Robert and Alicia ten-year prison sentences.

While still in county jail, awaiting final sentencing, Robert was visited regularly by a pastor who kept telling him about God's love and Jesus' desire to set him free. Robert would cuss and swear and verbally abuse the preacher, rejecting everything he had to say. One day, however the preacher showed up and said: "God is tired of knocking on your door and you not answering him." With a few more words indicating a life of eternal torment the preacher left. In the middle of the night, unable to sleep, Robert took out his Bible (one he had preciously requested because the pages of Bibles made good rolling paper) and began to read. There he came across these words: "Therefore, if anyone is in Christ, he is a new creation. The old has passed away; behold, the new has come. (2 Corinthians 5:17 ESV) Thinking of all the people and families he had hurt because of his actions and the drugs he had provided; Robert was thrilled to know the past could be left there and a fresh start was indeed possible. There on the floor of that filthy, desolate cell, Robert knelt, confessing his many sins, and seeking forgiveness from the One who makes all things new. Yes, he still had to face a mandatory three years of his ten-year sentence, but for the first time in his life, Robert was truly free.

While God was dealing with Robert, he was also working in Alicia's life so on March 9, 2002, Alicia woke in her prison cell and decided she was through running with the devil, raised her arms to heaven and gave it all over to God. Just as Robert needed the years of his prison sentence to find grounding in the Lord, so Alicia found women who mentored her in her faith and helped her grow as a Christian.

Robert and Alicia have been out of prison for ten years now and are part of Heaven's Saints Motorcycle Ministry. They have traveled and shared their testimony of God's changing and delivering grace, many times with prisoners behind the very bars where they once resided. But about five years ago, Robert was asked to consider a new and unique ministry opportunity.

Pilgrims Rest Baptist Church, which was officially recognized in 1881, was for many years a flourishing congregation but by early this century its numbers were dwindling, and it eventually closed its doors. Though some of the details are uncertain to me, Bob Johnson, the pastor of Alford Baptist suggested to Robert that the church be re-opened as a different kind of church, ministering to Bikers and the homeless. Thus, Heaven's Way Biker Church came to be with Robert and Alicia leaving their native Alabama to lead this unique ministry.

It was while I was visiting Bobby Wells (who's incredible testimony

I first read in a little newspaper published by Cochise and Set Free Church in Daytona) in Naples Florida, that he shared with me some videos of Heaven's Way and put me in touch with Robert. Though I was pleased with what I saw and heard from Bobby, I had no idea what I was riding into when I showed up in Cottondale. Bobby made a friend suggestion through Facebook so Robert and I connected and messaged beforehand, but I had no idea what to expect. The fact is, even if I had seen more pictures and had the opportunity to read the full history, nothing could have prepared me for what I found at Heaven's Way Biker Church.

Please allow me a few moments to refresh your memory and mine as to how I wound up at Heaven's Way Biker Church to begin with. I met Cochise in Daytona Beach and he suggested I stop in to see his friend Bobby Wells in Fort Myers when I was down that way. Bobby and his wife Michelle provided me a guest room in their home a few weeks later and Bobby told me about Robert Happoldt and HWBC. Now I had never met Robert but through Bobby's friend suggestion on Facebook, we shared a few messages. I had asked him if there was any place at the church where I might be able to hang my hammock or otherwise crash for the night as I came through the Florida panhandle, and he simply told me to call when I hit town.

As someone who has planted churches, worked with people with addictions and spent ten years running a transitional housing program for men in recovery, I think I have seen and experienced quite a few things that many pastors never do. Yet, nothing could have prepared me for what I found in Cottondale, Florida.

Having ridden all day on mostly backcountry roads from Daytona across the northern tier of Florida, I stopped in Tallahassee for the night and let Robert know I would be arriving some time on Saturday. He asked me if I preached and when I assured him I did, he simply said, "This Sunday 2PM Biker Church." That was my first clear sign, that this a faith-based ministry. Arriving in Cottondale, I called Robert for specific directions.

To get a general sense of things, one must understand that Cottondale, FL is a poor, rural community. Located roughly 80 miles west of Tallahassee and 40 miles south of Dothan, AL, the nearest city, Cottondale boasts a population of just over 900 residents with a median household income of less than $19,000 per year. To put that in perspective, the median household income for the state of Florida is a little over $45,000. These and other factors combine to make this community a natural breeding ground for alcohol and drug addiction along with the other social ills that normally accompany substance abuse.

The center of town lies about three miles off Interstate 10, and then Heaven's Way Biker Church is another six or seven miles out country roads at the end of the blacktop of Woodcrest Rd. As I pulled up, I found Robert, Wayne (who has been living at the church for almost two months and Nemo (a fellow sojourner, though traveling on two feet instead of two wheels) working out front, rebuilding the church sign. Robert greeted me, suggested I pull my bike around back, showed me where to put my things then went right back to work.

As soon as I unstrapped and stowed my gear, I went back out front with my camera to begin the important act of chronicling this place. After getting some initial shots I joined the work party, not because anyone said I should, it simply felt like the right thing to do. After painting and sealing the plywood, we mounted it to the framework over the old granite sign of Pilgrims Rest Baptist Church.

As dusk began to fall, we all headed inside, and I met more folks who were staying at the church. I met Tina who was traveling with Wayne from Indiana. John, a guy on a sport bike from South Carolina, and K.R., a Lakota Indian who for some reason found himself in crisis in Cottondale.

Alicia had come over and offered her greeting as well, then after digging out a bunch of food from the pantry and the refrigerators which Tina set to work turning into our dinner, Robert and Alicia went back across the road to the parsonage. Wayne has a job washing dishes at a little Mexican restaurant in town so Tina prepared dinner for the rest of us. Setting it all out on the counter, we gathered into a circle and held hands for the blessing, which was led by K.R.

As dinner drew to a close, people just started getting up and taking care of cleanup. I have been in churches where everyone knows each other and knows their way around the various tasks that need to be performed, but I have never seen anything go smoother in my life. Here we were, five travelers from very different backgrounds, on separate journey's working in near perfect harmony. As the newest "member of the family" I assumed they had been working together this way for a long time, only to discover that K.R. and John had only been around for a week and Nemo for two with Tina (and Wayne) the longest in residence at about 8 weeks. I felt so welcome, so comfortable, so at ease that I knew instantly, only the Holy Spirit can bring this kind of unity amongst veritable strangers

Over the next couple of days, I had the opportunity to get to know these folks a little better. Unfortunately, K.R. was suffering with a terrible toothache due to a lost filling and slept most of the time I was there so I didn't get much of his story, but this much I came to understand. He was a traveler in need, was provided food and shelter along with a scheduled dental appointment to address his most pressing need. He was loved and welcomed and grateful in return.

John had been traveling for some time but apparently found himself out of funds to continue his journey. Finding HWBC as a temporary home he went out in search of work and found employment as a cook at a Waffle House in Dothan. Since he was off to work a great deal of the time I was around, I didn't get to know him as well as I would have liked but the gist I got was that he was doing all he could to provide for himself and was looking for a place closer to work where he could settle in for a while.

Nemo, as I said was on a walking trip from Indiana. He had set out to walk a thousand miles with his destination Saint Petersburg, FL Nemo is an artist who works with items he finds in nature. Along his journey he has created works of art that remain in place wherever he creates them. Some are made using fallen leaves, moss, and twigs, so when the wind blows, they are gone from view but not from memory, or in some cases a digital record. Similar to my own journey, Nemo's is deeply spiritual in nature, and it is his hope to publish his artful sojourn someday. After his R & R break at Heaven's Way, he plans to be back on the road soon for the last two to three hundred miles of his trek.

As often happens when people find out I am a pastor, Tina opened up to me about her troubled past. Though I want to be careful not to divulge anything that may have been spoken under the assumption of confidentiality, she admitted that leaving Indiana was like running away, something she needed to do to get her head on straight. She was so thankful to have found a place like HWBC where she found such peace. She told me that while she knew she couldn't stay forever, the notion of leaving this peaceful haven brought tears to her eyes.

Wayne had his own troubles back home; having lost much, he is fighting his own demons but looking to make a fresh start. With an appearance similar to Hulk Hogan and a down home Midwestern mindset he is undeterred by his circumstances. Working as a dishwasher in a local Mexican restaurant he has managed to convince his employer that he should pay him a salary and let him work whatever hours needed to get the job done. Thus, he goes into work for a couple of hours three times per day, doing morning prep, then cleanup after lunch and dinner. I have never seen anything quite like this arrangement but since it works well for both employer and employee, everyone is happy.

While each of my fellow travelers will testify to faith in Christ, none of them look or act much like the folks I have gone to church with over the years of my Christian walk. I would say with the certainty that none will not be offended by this, that they are all aware of their brokenness, comfortable with their imperfections and joyous in the knowledge that God loves them, cares for them and is at work in them, accepting them just the way they are. What made this brief encounter so thrilling for me was that not one of them was wearing a mask. There were no facades, no pretense, and no false holiness.

Aside from these fellow travelers, I found much the same in our host and hostess, Robert and Alicia, as well as all those who gathered for church, both Sunday morning in Alford, and Sunday afternoon in Cottondale.

While I may not have been everywhere and seen it all, over the years I have had opportunity to travel and visit many churches of various flavors and denominations, but I never seen anything like I did last weekend. In Alford, the sponsor church for Heaven's Way, I saw very traditional Southern Baptist ladies in dresses with classic church lady hairdo's worshipping side by side with tattooed women in jeans and black leather. I saw Southern gentlemen in coats and ties greeting and hugging long-haired, bearded bikers. In Cottondale, I saw many of these same people respond positively to a simple gospel message brought to them by a Yankee preacher. In other words, I witnessed what church growth experts have told me was impossible, but what I took as a foretaste of heaven.

Chapter 9

A Tale of Two Churches

C UB Houston

As I trust is coming through in some of my writings, my horizons were being expanded and my worldview was being reshaped on this trip. I met some people and attended some churches that were very different than my rather traditional white, middle-class history. Though traditional, I have always considered myself open-minded. I know some who know me well, including my children may laugh at that notion, but it is true. It is entirely possible to be open-minded, yet conservative and opinionated. Now, stop laughing, I have something very important to share with you all.

Following my time at Heaven's Way Biker Church I began my westward journey. By the following Sunday I had been settled in for a few days in Baton Rouge, LA and since I hadn't come across anything unique looking, decided to attend the local church of my denomination. Being in Baton Rouge, I expected a church of some diversity, instead I found a church that epitomized white middle class-ness, and I felt oddly uncomfortable. Why? I wondered. Here was a church that not too many years ago I might have dreamed of pastoring. The people were friendly, the music was familiar, I knew when to stand, when to sit and how to behave at the artificially friendly greeting time. I'll admit, I was a bit underdressed in jeans and a t-shirt but as I thought about it, I knew that wasn't the cause of my discomfort. Was it that feeling of being an outsider? Well, sort of, but then again, I have been an outsider everywhere I have been on this trip. The thing is I didn't feel like an outsider in those other places, only here. Then it hit me, just how artificial, plastic and contrived it all felt to me. I feel terrible even saying this because I believe the people were basically sincere in their worship, or wanted to be at least, but couldn't see just how programmed they were. It was so much like I had grown up with, yet it left me cold. Cold isn't even adequate – more like frostbitten. When church was over, I couldn't get outside to the fifty-degree dampness fast enough, just to warm up a little.

I considered writing a post just about this experience but remembered the adage on which I grew up; "If you don't have anything nice to say, don't say anything at all." So, I held my tongue (or fingers if you will) and refrained. However, my experience the following Sunday has caused me to realize that sometimes you must call out the cold deadness. Even Jesus declared: "Woe to you, teachers of the law and Pharisees, you hypocrites! You are like whitewashed tombs, which look beautiful on the outside but on the inside are full of the bones of the dead and everything unclean. In the same way, on the outside you appear to people as righteous but on the inside you are full of hypocrisy and wickedness." (Matthew 23:27-28) Perhaps that quote is a bit strong for what I experienced, as I don't think the folks at that church were quite as dead in their faith as were the Pharisees, but if they do not wake up, they will be soon.

As I progressed through the next week, I continued to find myself battling unseasonably cold weather in Texas. Seriously, who would have thought I would need to wear the arctic rated underwear, I normally use when hunting in New England for a few days of camping in South Texas? Perhaps the physical cold and its attending misery are symbolic of everything I want to leave behind that is less than genuine in terms of my Christian faith.

Now we come to Church Under the Bridge. A slight misnomer, as the church no longer meets under the bridge, but it's where they started. However, the bridge in question is part of a busy interchange and the crowds grew too large, so for safety reasons the city asked them to find another location to meet. Today, the church meets in a field owned by another church not far from the bridge.

I had discovered this church online, while researching another church in Waco that I was planning to visit. All I had was an address, which I plugged into my iPhone setting off from my campsite about 42 miles south. Not knowing exactly where I was going, I left plenty early. When my phone indicated that I had arrived at my destination I found nothing to indicate that I was where I wanted to be. Since this location also happened to be on the edge of Houston's Third Ward, ranked number fifteen in the most violent neighborhoods in America, I knew it was not where I wanted to be without a clear purpose for being there.

I headed off in search a friendly and safer feeling place and found a Starbucks (yes, I understand that my white middle class-ness is shining through) several blocks away. I accessed the web to make sure I had the address correct and according to the ministry's website, 1000hills.org, I was indeed in the right place, so after a quick cup of coffee, I headed back. Upon my return I found a small group setting up for church.

Out of a van and small trailer, emerged a generator, a portable sound system and laptop computer, several portable instant canopies, stacks of plastic chairs, a few folding tables, a large cross and an a-frame sign that simply read, CHURCH – EVERYONE WELCOME. I have done church planting on a shoe-string budget before, but this whole packaged church, which by-the-way is set up and taken down in this location, 7 days per week, I would ballpark at about a $10,000 cost, including the van and trailer. I tracked down the pastor to introduce myself and ask permission to take pictures. He greeted me warmly and told me to feel free to take all the pictures I wanted.

It was a cold, rainy day, which I know affects church attendance anywhere, but I assumed one that met outdoors might be particularly impacted. The seats were better than 80% filled, (which church growth experts say is full, since people prefer a little personal space. Ah, see how they love one another.) I estimated the crowd at 60 to 70 but the pastor told me they usually run closer to 90 to 100 at every service. Again, that's not just this Sunday afternoon service, but they meet in this same spot Monday through Saturday at 7:00 pm. Furthermore, this same ministry hosts Church in the Park, Wednesday through Saturday at 9:30 am, and Church in the Driveway, Monday through Friday at 7:30 am and Sunday at 10:00 am. The Driveway Church by-the-way meets in the driveway to their Disciple Houses program, which rather than trying to describe myself, I will just share this statement from their website: "Our Disciple Houses are a residential living program for men working to get off the streets, who accept Jesus Christ as Savior and have a burning desire to serve God and work hard. The men are trained and discipled to work in the ministry, or receive support in learning skills for secular jobs."

So, did you catch those numbers? This ministry is conducting 18 Bible preaching church services every week! Plus running a discipleship housing program as well as planting churches in Latin America, Columbia, Africa and elsewhere around the globe. Oh, guess what else. At every one of those services, they serve a meal to everyone who comes!

This place is the real deal, this is Christianity in action

Earlier in this chapter I was pretty harsh concerning the church I visited in Baton Rouge, but I believe with good reason. You see, several times now on this journey I spoke at length with people who have a Christian background and who quite willingly told me that they still believe, yet for a variety of reasons, they have become disenfranchised from the church of their youth. Some told me that the church has become too political; others said the church is all about money or about power or cite the issues of child abuse and molestation among the clergy. Still others declare it's just so empty and irrelevant to their daily lives. They told me they are sick of the prosperity gospel or the feel-good gospel and are hungry to be challenged and called to something more meaningful.

So, it is with the Holy Spirit's conviction in my own heart that I say to all churches that are just happily going through the motions, providing services to the people who are already in, but doing little to meet the temporal and spiritual needs of those without, it is time to wake from your slumber! It is high time you/we start reflecting the nature and character of the Christ who is revealed to us in Scripture, for we are called to be his ambassadors, not his gatekeepers.

When I review the history of the many denominations, I find many were very different in their early days from what they have become today. I remember distinctly during my preparation for ministry a class in which we discussed the life span of a movement. I don't claim to be an expert on organization lifespans but here is what I remember from our discussions and personal study.

Everything starts with an idea. When an idea is shared and embraced by others, if it significant enough to create action, then two or more people band together to create a movement. As the movement gains momentum and grows in the number of participants, while it may seek to avoid the trappings of an institution, it soon becomes clear that without some sort of structure it becomes chaotic and ineffective. Thus, rules and some forms of organizational authority are developed. Over time, as the organization continues to grow and diversify, the original catalytic idea or ideal is all too easily forgotten. It is at this stage that the organization has become an institution. Institutions become their own life form and rarely look anything like the original idea or movement.

Now, let me share with you the words of Dr. Phineas F. Bresee, a Methodist minister of the late 1800's who along with his friend Dr. J.P. Widney and eighty additional charter members, started the movement that became the Church of the Nazarene: "We were convinced that houses of worship should be plain and cheap, to save from financial burdens, and that *everything should say welcome to the poor.* We went feeling that *food and clothing and shelter were the open doors to the hearts of the unsaved poor,* and that through these doors we could bear to them the life of God. We went in poverty, to give ourselves – and what God might give us – determined to forego provision for the future and old age, in order to see the salvation of God while we were yet here. God has not disappointed us. While we would be glad to do much more, yet hundreds of dollars have gone to the poor, with loving ministry of every kind, and with it a way has been opened up to the hearts of men and women, that has been unutterable joy. The gospel comes to a multitude without money and without price, and *the poorest of the poor are entitled to a front seat at the Church of the Nazarene,* the only condition being that they come early enough to get there." [1](Emphasis mine)

The movement that began nearly 120 years ago is now an institution. I am happy to report that there are still Nazarene churches that reflect the work and ideals of the original movement, but I fear they are too few and certainly not the norm.

I pray that by now I haven't bored you to tears with sociology and griping. All the above I feel was necessary to set the stage for what I witnessed and experienced at Church Under the Bridge.

Again, I found a small team at work setting up church, where just a few short minutes prior, had been a vacant lot in an impoverished and dangerous neighborhood in Houston. While there were a few volunteers from a supporting church or ministry, the majority of the work was being done by those who had been reached through the ministry of the church and were enrolled in the discipleship program.

As the time for service drew near, one could see the congregation gathering, shuffling in from all points of the compass. They were all dressed in multiple layers, with several sporting black plastic trash bags as their outerwear, hoping for some measure of protection from the rain. Most carried small backpacks with the remainder of their worldly goods. A few rode bicycles but the majority were truly pedestrian. Just as the make-up of the neighborhood is predominantly African American, so were those present, with a few of apparent Hispanic origin and perhaps three white guys. Needless to say, this white guy, with the silver reflective strips on his motorcycle jacket, moving around snapping pictures of everyone and everything kind of stood out. Yet, I felt less like an outsider here amongst the homeless than I had in that comfy church in Baton Rouge.

As we huddled together under the pop-up awnings the worship service began with prayer and readings from both the Old and New Testaments. Then the guest speaker, Tyrone Obaseki, was introduced and he stepped forward. Here was another who appeared almost as out of place as I. He was dressed in fine clothes with a black trench coat and sweet black fedora. He stepped to the pulpit and blew a Yemenite Shofar, something that has become popular in some circles as a call to worship, signifying a call to battle or spiritual warfare.

Tyrone spoke to the men (and few women) with boldness and authority, declaring their need to choose whether to continue down a path of destruction and despair through drug abuse or to turn away from sin and turn to Jesus as the solution. He was open and honest about his own past, having been raised in the foster care system from infancy to adulthood, experiencing homelessness and drug addiction firsthand. He had been in their shoes yet found deliverance and had no problem calling them to repentance.

Following the message, pastor Kenneth stepped forward and reinforced the call to repentance, challenging all present to choose the better way of Christ and specifically inviting them to join in a prayer of repentance if they chose to turn things around. After that we huddled together to celebrate the Lord's Supper. Several chairs were removed to allow folks to come forward to receive the elements. The pastor encouraged everyone to gather close, as communion is a special family time and so we all stood, shoulder to shoulder with wafer and cup in hand, joining together in the Lord's Prayer. As I stood in this throng, repeating those familiar words that I have uttered countless times in my life, I found myself moved to tears. I didn't understand why then and have thought about it several times since. Perhaps it was merely being in the presence of many for whom "daily bread" is an earnest concern. Perhaps, if I am totally honest, I felt a slight sense of superiority and was feeling grateful for the privileged life I have been given.

In my final analysis, however, while both of the above were factors in my emotions, I am convinced it was the hardships I had faced in the years leading up to that journey along with the minor deprivations I had experienced along the way that caused me to truly hallow my God. To know that he knows my needs and promises to meet them daily, that he calls me to extend forgiveness, just as I have received it from him. Understanding that he desires to set me free from all evil and that every aspect of that familiar prayer is possible because Jesus, a man without sin, became sin for me, paying my debt on Calvary.

The conclusion to this Tale of Two Churches is simply this: For me, Church Under the Bridge did far more in helping me to see the face of Christ and is a better representation of my own church's heritage and the New Testament ideals to which I believe we are all called, than the comfy, cozy suburban church that has become so much of mainstream Christianity.

Here is the call of God that Bresee was anxious to extend to all he met:
   "Come unto me, all ye that labour and are heavy laden, and I will give you rest.
   Take my yoke upon you, and learn of me; for I am meek and lowly in heart: and ye shall find rest unto your souls.
   For my yoke is easy, and my burden is light." (Matthew 11:28-39 KJV)

May the western church wake from its slumber and extend this call once again!

48

Chapter 10

Lost and Found

Mark Thomas Redwine

"If I were you, I wouldn't do it." So said a pastor with experience helping to plant churches in Mexico, in response to my inquiries regarding where to go and what to look for concerning the Church south of the border. He went on to explain that what we were seeing in the media is just the tip of the iceberg when it comes to kidnappings, beheadings, and disappearances.

I took his counsel to heart but couldn't shake a sense that my search would be incomplete without gaining some understanding of the spiritual climate and the workings of the church in this portion of North America. Sitting in my campsite at Lake Corpus Christi I was praying once again and asking God to lead me to my next stop. With more rain on the way I logged on to Priceline to see if I could find a cheap hotel for a couple of days around Brownsville, Texas. Low and behold, I found a room on South Padre Island that was cheaper than my campsite. What's not to love about the off-season?

These were not high-class accommodations, but I was warm and dry and closer to the border. After a couple of days of searching, sending emails to churches explaining my quest and getting no response, I was about to give up and start heading back north but decided to check one last resource. I surfed over to www.nazarene.org and typed Brownsville, TX into the church finder box. What do you know, up popped a work called "Lost and Found" – there was no website for the church, just an email address, but intrigued by the name I fired off a quick message and went to get some coffee. By the time I got back to my room I had a response from Pastor Mark and after exchanging a couple more emails we made plans to meet for dinner at Kiki's Restaurant Familiar. This was no Tex-Mex joint, but a true Mexican restaurant. Over a simple dinner, Mark and Marilyn Redwine became almost instant friends and I knew that God had led me to kindred spirits.

Mark explained that this was a different kind of work ministering exclusively to the local Mexican population most of whom live in the Colonias (A Colonia is a semi-rural subdivision of substandard housing lacking basic physical infrastructure, potable water, sanitary sewage, and adequate roads.) in the area. Before we parted for the night, he invited me to bring the message at their Thursday evening service.

Thursday morning, I awoke, giving thanks to God for providing an opportunity to gain the knowledge I sought without the risks associated with riding my bike into Mexico. I must admit that I also began my day with a certain amount of trepidation. Thus far on this trip I had found wonderful ministries serving the homeless, addicts and those with physical and developmental disabilities. Out of the box ministries for sure, but I have a fair amount of experience with these populations. Then there were the Biker churches, again, different, but as a guy touring North America on a motorcycle, those are folks with whom I have shared interest. However, with the Mexican immigrant population I had no previous exposure, nor even a point of reference.

I prayed; "God, what do I, a middle-class gringo who's running all over the place on a motorcycle have to share with these folks?" His answer: "You have me, you have the story of what I am doing in your life, and you have a desire to learn from them. What more do you need?" With that clarity, I spent a little more time in preparation and enjoyed the rest of my day.

As evening approached, I headed to Mark and Marilyn's house, having agreed to meet there so I could ride with them into the Colonia. There I met Karen, a teenager from another Colonia who spends a good deal of time at the parsonage and serves as a backup translator at times. Then Ron and Kay showed up, they're a wonderful couple called in retirement to offer themselves as volunteer missionaries. As we headed out to the van we were joined by "Granny", the widow of a Mexican pastor/church planter who lives next door to the parsonage, and what I assumed was her real-life grandson.

After a short drive we arrived at the mobile home where the meeting is held each week. Mark explained that the deck on which we met was fairly new. When services started at this location the deck was small and rickety and the only thing steady was the fear that it would collapse at any moment. A work and witness team from another church came down and built this new deck so the group would have a safe place to meet.

There were about twenty of us on the deck Thursday night, with temperatures in the fifties and a steady twenty mph wind, gusting at times to about twice that speed. Most folks were dressed in layers and bundled up against the cold yet, undeterred. Since none of these homes have heat, they are quite used to dressing for the cold.

After a few songs, a couple in English but most in Spanish, requests and concerns were shared and Granny led in prayer. Mark stood to introduce me to the congregation, saying he felt like we had been friends for years (the Bible does say that "with the Lord a day is like a thousand years") and invited me to share a little of my story.

Working with an interpreter, I shared J.I. Packer's quote that Christianity in North America is three thousand miles wide and a half-inch deep and went on to explain my search for deeper pools of authentic faith. I was just beginning to feel like the interpreter and I were getting into a pretty good rhythm when I made the statement that though I had been in ministry for almost thirty years, I had seen far too few people radically transformed after coming to know God. What happened next was absolutely precious, for instead of translating, my interpreter looked at me with shock and simply said, "You haven't?" Suddenly, it was as if everyone else disappeared and the two of us engaged in a dialogue about how while I had seen some people dramatically changed as a result of their relationship with God, the vast majority of Christians I know are pretty much the same as people in the world, with only slightly different priorities. She then turned and attempted to explain to everyone else what we were discussing. Based on the looks on all their faces, it seems the gist of what I was trying to convey came across.

I went on to share the story of the two disciples on the original Emmaus Road journey and how their eyes were opened, and their hearts burned within them when they encountered the risen Christ.

While I was pleased to be able to share with these folks, I am certain that

I received the greater blessing in observing their faith and fellowship. It was genuine and not in the least dependent on their circumstances. As a result, I decided to stick around Brownsville for a few more days, moving out of my hotel and into a guest room at the parsonage where Mark and Marilyn were extremely gracious hosts.

The story of my time in Brownsville, (almost Mexico) TX would not be complete without sharing a little more about the wonderful man of God who is leading this amazing work.

Prior to moving to Brownsville to plant this church, Mark Thomas Redwine was a Chiropractor living in Butte, Montana. As a Nazarene layman, Mark had traveled to Africa several times on short- and medium-term missions trips serving in a variety of ways as he was led by God. Each time he returned to the states he was able to rebuild his practice and get his patients back. Yet, after his last trip to Africa the Chiropractic practice didn't recover so well and it became clear that God had other plans.

Years earlier, Mark said he felt God had called him to plant a Spanish speaking church; however, one does not find a large ethnic population in Butte, MT. He would go to Wal-Mart and Home Depot scanning the faces of the crowds looking for people with brown eyes and slightly darker skin, to no avail. So, it was that at the age of sixty-three, through those connections built during years of missions trips, Mark was prepared to respond to the opportunity to move to South Texas as part of the Nazarene Border Initiative and plant that Spanish speaking church.

With limited financial support, Mark's days are filled with pastoral duties, compassionate ministry food and clothing distribution and a part-time job, as he puts it, pounding dents out of trumpets. In fact, Mark repairs musical instruments of all kinds in order to put food, not only on his table, but often, on the tables of the people to whom he has been called to serve.

Yes, indeed my friends, God led me to another place where Christianity is far more than a half-inch deep.

Chapter 11

Mission Waco – Mission World

J immy Dorrell

I went to Waco because I ran into someone in Cottondale, FL who told me about Church Under the Bridge, which sounded intriguing to me. What I found was far more than a unique church, though that in and of itself is very cool and you can read all about it in the next chapter. In addition, I found a Christian Community Organization called Mission Waco – Mission World that operates over two-dozen programs for adults, teens, and children. I had the opportunity my first night in town to attend their annual banquet, and the next morning sat with the founder, Jimmy Dorrell, who offered me a quick overview then handed me off to an Executive Assistant who took me around town to tour several of their facilities and programs.

The scope of this ministry is almost overwhelming, addressing a myriad of social ills with a distinctly Biblical approach. Even as I write that phrase, I cringe to think of what that might mean to those of you who read it. Some will think, "Great, they preach the Gospel and tell people about Jesus, because Jesus is the answer!" Others will surmise: "Oh great, they just preach at people and tell them if they don't clean up their acts, they will go to hell." Still others might assume this is some type of modern Robin Hood-ery, taking from the rich and giving to the poor, an effort to "redistribute wealth" under a Christian cloak. But the truth is, a Biblical, Christ-like response to poverty, hunger, homelessness, addiction, education, and commerce is very different from any of the above.

Repeatedly the Bible instructs us to follow the heart of God who cares for the poor. In the law, God instructed the harvesters not to harvest completely in either field or vineyard, in order that the poor and needy would have opportunity to gather for themselves'.

Following his baptism and wilderness temptation, Jesus entered the Temple in his hometown and read these words found in the book of Isaiah:

"The Spirit of the Lord is on me,
   because he has anointed me
   to proclaim good news to the poor.
   He has sent me to proclaim freedom for the prisoners
   and recovery of sight for the blind,
   to set the oppressed free,
   to proclaim the year of the Lord's favor."
   Then sat down and said: "Today this scripture is fulfilled in your hearing." (Luke 4:18-21)

If God, the Father, instructs us to care for the poor, the widow, the orphan and the alien, and God the Son declares that the Spirit anointed him to proclaim good news, freedom, recovery and favor to the poor, prisoners, blind and oppressed, then I suppose we, who bear his name and are called to be his ambassadors ought to pay attention and follow his lead. And that's exactly what the programs and services of Mission Waco are designed to do.

According to their Mission Statement, they: *Provide Christian-based holistic, relationship-based programs that empower the poor and marginalized. Mobilize middle-class Americans to become more compassionately involved among the poor. Seek ways to overcome the systemic issues of social injustice which oppress the poor and marginalized.*

Following an empowerment model of care, all those who receive services are encouraged to accept and grow in responsibility. Though space does not allow for all details, nor do I desire to bore my readers, let me summarize with the following: In most of the programs that might be free elsewhere, there is a small, manageable fee for services that increases as time goes on. For instance, in the homeless shelter, the first three nights are free. On nights four through thirty, there is a $2.00/night charge which increases to $5.00 for nights thirty-one through sixty-three, at which time the expectation is that the person is moving on or moving up to a different type of program.

I originally wrote the contents of this chapter sitting at the counter of the World Cup Café, a quaint 45-seat restaurant operated by Mission Waco, which declares they are "changing the world one cup at a time, while remembering fair trade for a fair world." Attached to the restaurant is the Fair-Trade Market, which sells a wide variety of jewelry, clothing, and crafts, created by artisans from around the world now earning a living wage.

This whole organization came to be when Jimmy and Janet Dorrell, understanding God's call to incarnational ministry bought a home in a blighted neighborhood in North Waco. As I gleaned from conversations with a few people, this area was previously a well to do primarily Jewish neighborhood. Over time it became a poor, mostly black neighborhood and now, thanks to incarnational ministry and the growth of Mission Waco, it is a racially and ethnically diverse neighborhood.

The building that houses the café and market is also the location of the administrative offices and sandwiched between the two is the Jubilee Theater, which was formerly a porn house, and now hosts productions with a Christian and/or socially conscious message. Some of those very productions are written and prepared by staff and youth at the Youth Center the next building down. There, area youth gather Monday through Thursday afternoon for a time of Bible Study, fun tutoring, music, and learning. There is a fully equipped sound studio where the kids are able to produce hip-hop music. Down the block and around the corner we find yet another building, this one offering after school programs for kids ages four to eleven.

All that I share here, just barely scratches the surface of what Mission Waco is doing in this community. The truth is that while I keep mentioning Mission Waco, their full name as noted earlier, is Mission Waco – Mission World for they have programs and services in Mexico City, India, and Haiti as well. At the banquet I attended they promoted a project they were undertaking in the fall of 2015 to bring solar lighting to an entire village in Haiti. With no electricity in this village the primary home light source is kerosene lamps. Medical research has shown that breathing the soot produced by these lamps is equivalent to smoking two packs of cigarettes per day. These solar lights will not only resolve this health issue but will provide lengthened study time for students eager to learn.

Of all the things that amazed me about this place that so marvelously reflects the nature and character of Christ, I think what amazed me most is that I had never heard of it before arriving. This ministry should be more widely known, studied, and perhaps replicated in community after community around the United States. Jimmy and his crew offer trainings on a regular basis, hosting people from all over the world with that goal in mind. I urge you to check it out for yourself at www.missionwaco.org.

Chapter 12

A Slice of Heaven

Church Under the Bridge

Beneath Interstate 35, between 4th and 5th streets in Waco, TX, sits an egg-shaped island of concrete covering about ¾ of an acre. Most days it's just a vast oval of cement but come Sunday morning it is transformed into a little slice of heaven.

Vans and pick-up trucks pulling trailers that have been fitted for special purposes begin pulling up on this island an hour or two after sunrise. Out come the portable stage, sound system and instruments for the worship team. Off another trailer with custom racks come the metal folding chairs for the congregation and plastic tables for the meal to be served by a visiting church from the region. Nearby the serving tables one finds a few more tables where those who desire can sign up for small groups or grab helpful resources and information or buy their very own Troll t-shirt. At yet another set of tables one might find a youth group from another area church preparing to pass out fresh fruit and water.

As it becomes obvious that a gathering is going to take place more vehicles begin to arrive. Cars, trucks, motorcycles, and scooters begin to line the outer edge of the island and pull under the shelter of the southbound lane of the highway. As space becomes scarce, folks start parking in a vacant lot across the street or along the side streets to the east and west. Before you know it, people (and a few dogs) who have driven, ridden, and walked are gathered as the body of Christ.

While many churches may have a sign in front of their' buildings indicating that "All Are Welcome", few appear to believe that. However, the people gathered under the bridge seem to know this fact without any sign telling them so. Those who've come together represent all social and economic strata. There are plenty of middle-class looking people one might find in your average church, more than a few rough looking bikers, those clearly down on their luck and homeless struggling to survive, alongside corporate executives, business owners and other people of means. Throw in a few college students and professors from nearby Baylor University and consider that in each of the above categories one finds every shade of skin color and we indeed find a little slice of heaven. Or at least, what heaven will look like one day, for those who have put their trust in the atoning sacrifice of Jesus, the Christ.

Having reached the approximate halfway point in my planned journey, both in terms of time and miles, I found I had been blessed in ways I never would have imagined. In almost every state or region I had been, I found some deep, deep pools, where people of faith, acting in obedience to the Word of God and His will as it has been revealed to them, were and are marvelously impacting the communities around them and reflecting the nature and Character of Christ.

While I had many miles to go and many more regions to explore, I had a slight fear I may have peaked here in Waco. Between all the programs of Mission Waco, the incredibly authentic Church Under the Bridge and the cooperation from other churches in the city, I doubted I could find anything that better represented what I set out to find.

That statement should not detract in any way from any other people I met or places I had been, it is simply a fact that almost everything I hoped to experience came together in Waco.

Though the opening paragraphs of this chapter might give you a limited picture of what you would find if you were to make the journey to Waco yourself, let me take a few minutes now to share the stories of some of the people I met who have been touched by this church without walls.

Because Jimmy introduced me at the Friday breakfast and again from the platform on Sunday several people came up to me to chat face-to-face. Many were interested in the story of my trip but others were anxious to share with me the impact this church had in their lives.

When I shared with one man that I had been the director of a transitional housing program for men in recovery, he said, "Oh cool, I'm in recovery." He then went on to share the heartbreaking story of his downfall and his journey back. Fourteen years earlier his ten-year old daughter was raped, beaten, and killed. The shock, pain and emotional upheaval of this tragic loss were too much for him to bear. He began to drink heavily and when the alcohol could not numb his feelings he turned to drugs and then more drugs and more booze and anything at all that might provide a moment or two in which his tortured mind didn't picture her beaten body.

Living in an almost constant stupor, going to church didn't even enter his mind. Then one day, about five years prior to our meeting, he happened across this open-air church. No one seemed to look down on him in his inebriated state. Instead, he found a place of welcome and love and slowly began to realize that there was a better way and that he could move on with his life. He didn't act like suddenly everything was better, but over time he found new ways to cope and a glorious new life in Christ.

At the ball field Sunday afternoon (It just so happened that the Sunday I visited was the church's annual "Toilet Bowl" touch football game and Chili Cook-off) another man approached me to wish me well on my journey and told me the story of his family moving to Waco so they could be a part of this church. He explained that his son was born with developmental disabilities and as a Christian family they tried to live their lives as normally as they could, continuing to attend their church and treating their son with respect and dignity. As the boy grew, however, they found it hard to keep him still and quiet during service. He would get up and wander about and occasionally try to walk up on the platform and grab a microphone. One day the pastor spoke rather harshly to him, and while he could understand that his son might cause others to be distracted, he felt hurt and dejected.

On a visit to Waco, the family attended Church Under the Bridge. Though many are seated and focused on the music and the message, there are still quite a few people who are milling around during the service, so the boy was not alone in his wanderings and not the distraction he was considered in his home church. At one point the boy's wandering led him to the edge of the stage and he headed for the stairs to climb on up. As his father dashed to stop him, Janet, the pastor's wife, and worship leader said, "It's okay, he can come up here if he wants to."

Imagine the feelings that rushed through that father. The son that he loved was not seen as a distraction or a nuisance or a problem, instead he was accepted and welcomed. Immediately the family began to make plans to move to Waco.

A woman I bumped into in the parking lot told me how she had been a member of a fairly fundamentalist church and didn't really fit in. She tried another church that was a little less dogmatic and for a time felt comfortable, but subsequent moves and a search for another church where she felt she belonged proved difficult and she was about ready to give up on church altogether. Then she found Church Under the Bridge, where the Bible is not only preached, but is also lived out effectively in the context of community. Today she is a small group leader within the church and loving every minute of it.

These are just three quick snippets of what I have a very strong notion, represent dozens of similar stories that could be told were one to stick around Waco for any length of time. Part of me would have love to do just that; hang my hat in Texas for a while and learn these stories firsthand, but to paraphrase my fellow Granite Stater Robert Frost.

"The church is lovely, bright, and deep,
   But I have promises to keep,
   And miles to go before I sleep,
   And miles to go before I sleep."

Chapter 13

Truth or Consequences

As you just read, I concluded the previous chapter talking about plans for a much longer trip and a large part of me hopes someday to complete the four corners of the United States on my bike and gain new, interesting stories and insights. However, as I was traveling, my then still teenaged daughter was at home by herself and apparently failed to keep tabs on the heating oil for the furnace. Pipes froze and burst and while I tried at first to deal with the insurance company and the work of mitigation and reconstruction it became clear that I needed to head on home. I had already spent four months on the road, and I was convinced that after Waco, where God had done an incredible work in my soul which I will share more about in chapter fourteen, The Biggest Lesson, and I was ready for a return to some form of normalcy. I had ridden on from Waco, across West Texas, through the oil fields and on into New Mexico and one of the last places I made camp was Truth or Consequences, New Mexico. It seemed a fitting place to end this journey and an appropriate title for this second to last chapter in the record.

Shortly before setting out on my journey, I attended a pastor's brunch and had the opportunity to share and pray with some ministerial colleagues. As I described my search for the reflection of Christ in postmodern North America, one of the men at my table noted that many sociologists and philosophers, say we are even beyond postmodernism and now into supermodernism or hypermodernism.

One of my discoveries on the road was that none of these terms or labels means a thing to the average man or woman on the street. However, before I dive into this lack of labeling or embracing of specific philosophies, let me step back a bit to explain why I adopted my premise and approach.

While the issue is more complex than the scope of this book, postmodernity has been used a great deal to give justification as to why the church has been losing ground in recent years. The gist of the rationalization goes something like this: In the "modern age" as technology progressed there was hope that everything would get better. That with advances in modern science man could figure out solutions to every problem and the world would experience a golden age of reason and greater enlightenment and peace. However, when man's overall condition failed to improve significantly, postmodernism declared that knowledge and truth are not discovered, rather they are invented. In other words, there is no such thing as truth. You can have your truth and I can have my truth, and anyone can have whatever truth they so choose. Thus, the rationale or the excuse used to explain why the church is losing congregants so rapidly is that people have rejected the truth claims of the church. While this may be a slight oversimplification of the matter, it is generally what I have heard for many years now and a presumption, which I had accepted prior to my Emmaus Road Trip.

Yet, as I continue to process the things I found and the conversations I had while on the road, it strikes me that no one challenged me with a denial of truth, or the truth claims of the church. Of the dozens of theological and intellectual exchanges I had with folks in a variety of settings, not a single soul said to me that the problem with the modern church is its insistence on a particular truth.

People told me that they felt the church is too focused on money or has become too political. Several people told me the church is run too much like a business and many told me that they have a problem with hypocrisy in the church. More than a few raised the issue of child molestation by Roman Catholic priests, (in fairness I must acknowledge that sexual deviation and sin are not exclusive to Roman Catholic clergy) and the far-reaching efforts to cover up such atrocities. Plenty of folks told me they feel the church is "out of touch" with the culture, but again, not a single person said the problem with the church is its position on truth.

Now that I have had time to digest and reflect, I think I have figured out why I didn't hear that complaint or criticism. I'm pretty sure it's because the church is not making truth claims. The sad fact is that so many of us who preach the gospel have been sold a bill of goods that says people reject claims about absolute truth and, therefore, in an effort to be more palatable we have removed such bold statements from our preaching. In fact, one comment that was made to me more than once is that the church seems to be trying to compete with modern forms of entertainment and church has become another show. Since it can rarely compete on an even footing with modern entertainment, it has become a bad show; offensive to those who go seeking truth, and laughable to those accustomed to high tech sound and special effects.

Some time ago I was listening to the radio (a habit I had gotten out of while on my trip since I don't have a radio on my bike) while driving with four wheels beneath me and caught an NPR story about the radicalization of American youth and those who are joining ISIS or other Jihadist groups. I know I have heard this before, but it really struck me, perhaps in light of my own discoveries, as I heard again that one significant reason young Americans are joining these groups is that they long for something to believe in, something greater than themselves that declares the way things ought to be.

Meanwhile the average evangelical church youth group brings a bunch of teens together to play silly games and listen to crappy, supposedly hip music with pseudo-Christian lyrics, trying desperately to entertain our kids to faith. What a pathetic and unbiblical methodology we employ to fulfill the great commission! We wring our hands at the fact that we are losing our youth and fail to see that they aren't abandoning faith; rather they are simply walking away from lame forms of so-called Christian entertainment. They are abandoning the church because we have not presented them with any truth(s) on which to build their lives.

In his letter to the church in Ephesus, Paul writes about spiritual warfare and the armor of God. (See Ephesians 6:10-20) As he begins to describe the armor he says, *"Stand firm then with the belt of truth buckled around your waist..."* Catch that? Truth is the first piece of armor Paul says we are to don, and with good reason. The belt of a Roman Centurion wasn't merely a strip of cloth or leather around the waist used to hold his pants up. Particularly true since they didn't wear pants, but that's beside the point. The belt was a wide piece of leather with straps that crisscrossed in the back and came up and over the shoulders, attaching again at the front and was the foundation on which other pieces of armor mounted. The breastplate, (which spiritually, Paul equates with righteousness) designed to protect the vital organs, especially the heart, hung from hooks or buckles on the shoulder straps of the belt. In similar fashion the scabbard for the warrior's sword hung from this belt.

Without the belt of truth there can be no righteousness for without truth there is no foundation for righteousness! Without the belt of truth there is no place to mount one's sword and since Paul says the *"sword of the spirit which is the word of God"* we are left with nothing to offer that is different or greater than the philosophies of the world. Sure, we may be able to wear the "helmet of salvation" independent of the "belt of truth" but we are extremely vulnerable and thus weak and prone to injury, which I fear describes the condition of the average churchgoer these days.

Is the church losing ground? Yes, of this fact there can be little doubt. Are we losing ground because people have rejected our claims about truth? I think not. Rather, in our race to be relevant we've become less so, offering cheap grace in an inferior package. As one apologist I heard a short time ago said: "Most preaching today is nothing more than feel good pop psychology with a little Christian wording thrown in."

Lest you think I am about to break into a chorus of "Gimme that old time religion, Gimme that old time religion, Gimme that old time religion, it's good enough for me." please understand nothing could be farther from the truth. Old time religion was no better than new-fangled religion – I reject them both.

So, to my brothers and sisters, called of God to proclaim his Word and truth, I set forth this challenge and/or encouragement: Be bold! Declare truth! Punch up those sermons with proclamations of truth worth living and dying over. Not simply to be offensive but to make known the Christ who said, "I am the way and the truth and the life. No one comes to the Father except through me." Who taught "the way of God in accordance with the truth." (John 14:6) Who "Came down from the Father full of grace and truth." (John 1:14) Who said, "God is spirit and is worshippers must worship in Spirit and in truth." (John 4:24) And "If you hold to my teaching you are really my disciples. Then you will know the truth, and the truth will set you free." (John 8:31-32) And who prayed to the Father on our behalf, "Sanctify them by the truth; your word is truth." (John 17:17)

Now I pray that you will know the truth and find greater freedom in this life and the next, than you have ever experienced.

Chapter 14

Lessons Learned

For the past five plus years, I have been in a new pastorate in Seabrook, NH, seeking to apply a few things I learned over the 4 months and roughly 9,000 miles I traveled back in 2014/15 as I sought the reflection of Christ in postmodern North America.

To briefly recap, here's what I discovered. Despite the failings of many churches, God is still very much alive and thriving and so is His Church. While I had a few disappointing experiences, I seemed to tap into a vein of churches, what we might call church type missions, and para-church organizations where Christ was clearly manifest. These places were geographically, socio-economically, racially, and culturally diverse. Some were rather traditional, some served the homeless, some served a primarily immigrant population and others a particular sub-culture, yet in each of these places I saw the hands and feet of Christ at work, meeting needs and changing lives for the better.

Upon my return, I spent a great deal of time reflecting and analyzing, seeking to understand if there were certain common denominators in these vastly different ministries and environments. Initially I found three common factors: people and places where I felt no judgment upon myself or others, a strong emphasis on teaching the Word of God, and great fellowship or hospitality.

A few months ago, as I was considering a couple things, we were thinking of implementing in our church a fourth element came to mind. Perhaps I was a little slow to realize this because of the broken place I was in at the time, but it dawned on me that everywhere I felt the presence of God, I personally, was loved and accepted by those in leadership and beyond. Then, upon further reflection I saw one further factor. Each of these churches/ministries was "other focused." That is, they were all concerned with helping others and I can almost guarantee that the question, "What's in it for me/us?" was rarely, if ever, considered.

So, here's what I think is my conclusion on this whole thing about finding Christ, whether it be in postmodern North America or at any other time in history, or place in the world. Are you ready for this? I hope you're paying close attention because I think this is big. Simple, but big - so simple that I can't believe it's taken me this long to put it all together, but big enough to affect every ministry decision I expect ever to make.

The following summarizes what I learned on my quest: 1. The Word leads us to love God and love others. 2. It makes sense that fellowship/hospitality would follow because it's natural to want to spend time with those we love. 3. The Word teaches us that we have all fallen short, in other words we are all broken. If we recognize this truth about ourselves, then we must accept brokenness in others. 4. The Word teaches us to reach out and to consider others needs before our own. Perhaps to keep things even simpler we should see it like this:

1. A focus on The Word of God leads us to…
   a. Fellowship/Hospitality
   b. Acceptance of people where they are
   c. Focus on and concern for others.

If we have the first item right – the Word of God – then the items that follow are fluid in their order, yet one thing is critical, it's all about the Word of God. That must always come first in every consideration, because when the Word comes first, the other things flow from that. The Word teaches us that we must love God and love others. Our Jewish brothers and sisters are taught the Shema as the centerpiece of the morning and evening prayer service which includes the following passage: *"Hear, O Israel: The Lord our God, the Lord is one. Love the Lord your God with all your heart and with all your soul and with all your strength. These commandments that I give you today are to be on your hearts. Impress them on your children. Talk about them when you sit at home and when you walk along the road, when you lie down and when you get up. Tie them as symbols on your hands and bind them on your foreheads. Write them on the doorframes of your houses and on your gates."* (Deuteronomy 6:4-9) In the New Testament this command is tied to loving others by Jesus in several places, and best summarized in the parable of the good Samaritan found in Luke 10:25-37:

"On one occasion an expert in the law stood up to test Jesus. "Teacher," he asked, "what must I do to inherit eternal life?"

"What is written in the Law?" he replied. "How do you read it?"

He answered, "'Love the Lord your God with all your heart and with all your soul and with all your strength and with all your mind'; and, 'Love your neighbor as yourself.'

"You have answered correctly," Jesus replied. "Do this and you will live."

But he wanted to justify himself, so he asked Jesus, "And who is my neighbor?"

In reply Jesus said: "A man was going down from Jerusalem to Jericho, when he was attacked by robbers. They stripped him of his clothes, beat him and went away, leaving him half dead. A priest happened to be going down the same road, and when he saw the man, he passed by on the other side. So too, a Levite, when he came to the place and saw him, passed by on the other side. But a Samaritan, as he traveled, came where the man was; and when he saw him, he took pity on him. He went to him and bandaged his wounds, pouring on oil and wine. Then he put the man on his own donkey, brought him to an inn and took care of him. The next day he took out two denarii and gave them to the innkeeper. 'Look after him,' he said, 'and when I return, I will reimburse you for any extra expense you may have.'

"Which of these three do you think was a neighbor to the man who fell into the hands of robbers?"

The expert in the law replied, "The one who had mercy on him."

Jesus told him, "Go and do likewise."

Again, if we are living out these commands, then fellowship and hospitality naturally follow. It becomes an almost automatic byproduct of love.

When we understand the message of the Gospel, that we are all sinners in need of a Savior, we realize that we have no ground whatsoever to stand on, whereby we can judge others. Having had our sins forgiven, we are commanded to forgive others and it becomes natural to accept people the way Jesus does. Consider these words from the Apostle Paul to his friends in Philippi, "Therefore if you have any encouragement from being united with Christ, if any comfort from his love, if any common sharing in the Spirit, if any tenderness and compassion, then make my joy complete by being like-minded, having the same love, being one in spirit and of one mind. Do nothing out of selfish ambition or vain conceit. Rather, in humility value others above yourselves, not looking to your own interests but each of you to the interests of the others." (Philippians 2:1-4)

Just in case the point of being other focused isn't made clear in the above passages let's pick up the instruction that follows in Philippians 2:5-8, which was part of an early hymn of the church:

"In your relationships with one another, have the same mindset as Christ Jesus:
    Who, being in very nature God,
    did not consider equality with God something to be used to his own advantage;
     rather, he made himself nothing
    by taking the very nature of a servant,
    being made in human likeness.
     And being found in appearance as a man,
    he humbled himself
    by becoming obedient to death—
    even death on a cross!"

Did you catch that? Jesus, being in nature God, made himself nothing, took on the nature of a servant, and became obedient to the point of death. I promise you that at no time while Jesus contemplated the cross or prayed in the garden of Gethsemane, did he ever once say to his Father, "Okay, if I do this thing, what's in it for me?"

So, here's my new simple metric for ministry decisions. Is what we are considering clearly in line with the Word of God? If so, does it build fellowship, does it express Christ's acceptance or is it other centered? If we have a definite affirmative to the first as well as an affirmative to any of the following three elements, then we'll do it. Maybe not right away, since we might need to find and train leadership, but we will work to that end. If the answer is "no" to either question, we will pass.

Chapter 15

The Biggest Lesson

God's Love

I promised in chapter eleven that I would share more about the work God did in me while in Waco, yet I want to make clear that it didn't all take place in Waco, it was happening all along the way and simply became clearer and more settled at that point in my journey. Motorcycle riding requires more focused attention than driving a car. At the same time, it allows me to absorb my surroundings better and take in the sights (if you ride, I'm sure you know what I mean) affording me the opportunity to see things I have never seen before even when riding on the same road I may have driven many times before in an automobile. Furthermore, though I have Bluetooth in my helmet, I use it only for navigation, having chosen not to listen to music or podcasts or anything else, keeping my mind from distraction. Thus, even as I ride defensively, I can also process my thoughts on some of those long stretches of backroad or highway.

On day two of my trip, I was riding through Pennsylvania in steady rain; the temperature was hovering right around 40 degrees Fahrenheit and

I was battling heavily gusting winds; my gloves were soaked through, and my hands were almost numb and wanting to lock up around the handlebars. I began to pray as I road, questioning my own sanity and wondering if God had truly led me to undertake this search. Was He in this with me or was I completely out of my mind? God was silent at first, then suddenly, I felt warm at my core, and I thought to myself, I don't remember a time in my life that I have felt more alive. Lest you think that sudden warmth was a sure sign of hypothermia, understand, my body was still cold, but my heart was warmed, and I had God's assurance that I was on the right track.

I had many less than pleasant experiences and several cold receptions as I visited churches and ministry organizations along the way. Many times, I would pop into a church along my route in hopes of speaking to the pastor to share what I was doing and see if he had any recommendations of places to check out or people I should meet. I would often introduce myself as a preacher in exile, explaining that my wife had filed for divorce, my mother had died, my ministry had suffered and now I was on a spiritual quest. Many of those men looked across their desks at me as if I were the devil incarnate. They may have offered a platitude or two and false words of encouragement, yet it was clear they couldn't get me out of their office fast enough. Other times I would share my situation and the pastor would get up from his seat, come around his desk and give a hug, saying something to the effect of, "Oh brother, I am so sorry to hear what you are going through. I hope you know God has not abandoned you and please rest assured that I will be praying for you and your wife and family."

Somewhere along the road, after probably a half dozen or so of each type of reception, I was pondering the fact that there seemed to be no middle response, no sort of cold, no lukewarm, just genuinely warm, and encouraging or cold as ice. As I considered that, I flashed back to day two in the extreme cold of Pennsylvania and the warmth I experienced from God, and I was reminded again of just how much God loves me.

I pondered the immensity of God's love for me often along the way and was touched by the love I felt from folks like Ray and Susan, Cochise, Steve, Rico, Bobby, Robert and Alicia, Mark and Marilyn and many others that by the time I got to Waco, I was ready to believe deep down that yes indeed, God loves me.

At first glance, you might think that's a strange thing for me to state. How could a man who is a preacher, pastor, compassionate ministry director, not trust in God's love? I know, it seems dumb. I had preached many sermons about God's love for humanity. I had preached the cross of Calvary as a demonstration of His love. I had told people of God's love for them countless times and never doubted that on an intellectual level. I believed the evidence and knew it to be true!

BUT!

It was not until I was completely broken, until all the other things I had relied on and trusted in were stripped away and I realized that I brought absolutely nothing of value to the table that I was able to experience and accept God's love for me.

In the very first commandment God says, "You shall have no other gods before me." (Exodus 20:13) Well, I was familiar with that and knew it to be a truth, I had preached sermons against idolatry and warned others of the peril, yet subconsciously I had set up many idols in my own life. I didn't worship any of the common gods of this age such as fame or fortune. No, I was too smart to fall for those things that I know are fleeting. However, as I struggled with the shame of my failing marriage, I realized I was way too concerned with what people might think of me. In essence I had made my marriage an idol. I was a father of six wonderful children, we had sacrificed much so that Janet could be a stay-at-home mom and be free to homeschool our children and we were seen by many as a model family. I had made my family an idol. I was a good preacher and had been effective in leading a compassionate ministry to the homeless and addicted to more than double in capacity and had been seen by others as a community leader. My service and ministry had become an idol.

It wasn't until all those things I idolized had been stripped away and I was a lonely broken man on a quest for something deeper and more real that I was able to fully experience the agape love of God. The tears of repentance and joy flowed together, and I knew that no matter what else the future held, I am His and He is mine.

Epilogue

Much has happened in the five or six years since my journey of discovery and I don't want to leave you, my reader hanging with any sense of unfinished business so, let me take just a few more minutes of your time to bring you up to date.

First, on the Homefront: I wish I could tell you that when I came home from my trip, a repentant and changed man that suddenly everything fell into place and that my marriage was healed, my ministry restored and I had a George Bailey, It's a Wonderful Life, kind of ending. Alas, that was not to be. No, in fact, though we began to make peace Janet insisted on following through with divorce that had dragged on far too long, so on January 18, 2016, we signed papers and our marriage was legally dissolved. However, as I continued the work of rebuilding my life, Janet too had been figuring some things out and along about September, she called me one day and say that she too was sorry for all the pain and spoke the words I had so longed to hear, "I repent." We agreed to have dinner a few days later and over the next several weeks we continued to work through the things that had seemed so big, and we remarried on November 1, 2016.

Just five days later, with Janet by my side the fine folks of Rand Memorial Congregational Church in Seabrook, NH voted to take a chance on this broken man and called me to be their pastor, and on December 1, 2016, I was installed in this new roll. In these years since I have sought to employ the lessons learned on my Emmaus Road Trip shaping the church to be judgment free, focused on proclaiming the Word of God and making disciples. I'm happy to say the church has responded well and we are having the time of our lives!

Additionally, Janet and I started a ministry we call Covenant Shore, where we coach other couples who may be struggling to make their marriages healthier. Our hearts especially go out to clergy couples because so much is expected of us. Many pastors struggle with having a pastor's heart for their own families and pastor's families suffer from unrealistic expectations from congregations. If we can be of service to you, please reach out through our website www.covenantshore.org

Now some updates on some the people and ministries I have written about.

The Traversy family you met in chapter one has continued to flourish and grow. Genevieve is now a social worker and Foster Care Recruiter at Lutheran Services Carolinas. She and Shawn fostered and adopted a beautiful little girl and their entire family continue to be marvelous examples as they break the cycle of neglect and abuse. True reflections of Christ.

Sadly, Jakob's Well is no longer operational, but Ray and Susan Kelley continue to reach out to the hurting, homeless, addicted, and disaffected through Daytona Outreach Center. They shine as beacons of light in the darkness and serve as the hands and feet of Jesus. To get to know them and their work better, go to www.docdaytona.com

A year after we remarried, Janet and I took a trip to the Keys for a second honeymoon and happened to be in Big Pine Key on a Sunday morning.

We visited Keys Vineyard Church and renewed acquaintance with a few people, though we didn't find Rico. We headed on south to Key West for a few days and I managed to get ahold of Rico and schedule a time for the three of us to have lunch on our northward journey. At 75 he was still vibrant and still riding his Harley. If you make a trip to the Keys, be sure to visit this great church or watch online at www.keysvineyard.org

Jeremy Folmsbee remains in Daytona doing the work of making disciples, regularly posting beautiful pictures of the sunrise of Daytona Beach, and being an ambassador of Christ. Quiet and unassuming, you won't find a website for this church or any advertising anywhere, you just have to show up.

Cochise closed up shop at Set Free church and headed back to his native Kentucky for a time but apparently missed the sun and fun of Daytona Beach so he headed back down and continues to preach the gospel to anyone who will listen. You can often find him sharing Jesus at Boot Hill Saloon.

Church Under the Bridge and Church in the Driveway continues to offer services at two locations seven days per week and now has Church in the Office, their only indoor services twice a week. Near as I can tell, they have added two more Discipleship Houses since my visit. You can read more about this great ministry at www.1000hills.org

Mark Thomas Redwine has been extremely busy these days working to serve not only the people of the Colonias but ministering to the refugees and asylum seekers on both sides of the border. He and a band of helpers will load up little red wagons with food and other basic needs, pull them into Mexico and lead a worship service with his ukulele. Still no website but you can read more and keep up to date on their

Facebook page https://www.facebook.com/lostandfoundbrownsville/?ref=page_internal

Mission Waco has added several more programs to the over two dozen I was privileged to see. Jimmy has become the President Emeritus and brought in some young blood to continue the mission there and globally. Though I included the link in chapter Ten, here it is again www.missionwaco.org

Church Under the Bridge in Waco has had to temporarily relocate to the Magnolia Silos while as Jimmy puts it, The State of Texas completes the remodeling work on our sanctuary. A major widening of Interstate 35 is underway and is expected to be rather disruptive for some time. For more about their location and services browse on over to www.churchunderthebridge.org

Many of what is to be found in this book was written recently based on clear memories and a detailed journal I kept while I was traveling, some chapters, however, first appeared as blog posts which have been edited as they were originally written in the present tense. As it's all in the past now I tried to change the tense to make the story clearer – if you noticed any errors or found any of the timing confusing, please forgive me.

Finally, the lessons I learned, like so many lessons in life, were learned the hard way. The journey itself was both trying and joyous and it has taken me years to process it to the point where I felt ready to share it with the world. I hope and pray that you have learned something from my adventure and perhaps even been entertained. If you enjoyed the book or have gained any insight for yourself, I would very much appreciate it if you would leave a favorable review on Amazon.

Notes

CHAPTER 9

1   Gavin, E. A. (1982). *Phineas F. Bresee*. Nazarene Publishing House.

About the Author

Craig is the pastor of Rand Memorial Congregational Church in Seabrook, NH and a Certified Advanced Christian Life Coach. In addition to over 30 years of pastoral ministry and church planting, Craig has served as the Executive Director of Helping Hands Outreach Ministries and along with his wife, Janet, is the founder of Covenant Shore marriage coaching.